Presenting Professionally

Wow your audience, Win Hearts and Minds

By

George P Boulden

Edited by

Richard de Laat, CEO, Xiber Technologies GmbH
All Rights Reserved

No part of this book may be reproduced in any form,
by photocopying or by any electronic or mechanical means,
Including information storage or retrieval systems,
without permission in writing from both the copyright
owner and the publisher of this book
First Published October 2009

ALA INTERNATIONAL PUBLISHING

Lutterworth, England

Publisher email: alapub@ala-international.com

Email - george.boulden@ala-international.com

Web site - www.ala-international.com

Copyright © George P Boulden

Ed 10 August 2016

Contents

SYNOPSIS 3
ACKNOWLEDGEMENTS 4
PRESENTING PROFESSIONALLY- INTRODUCTION 6
   CHAPTER 1 - PLAN 8
      1.   Decide your purpose 8
      2.   Identify your audience 9
      3.   Define the context 10
      4.   Write your Script 11
      5.   Create Visuals 14
   CHAPTER 2 - REHEARSE 17
      1.   Learn your lines 17
      2.   Create the conditions 18
      3.   Rapport 18
      4.   Learn to manage the fear 22
      5.   Practice, Practice, Practice 23
      6.   Appearance 24
      7.   Create your environment 25
   CHAPTER 3 - DELIVER 27
      1.   Start by telling them what you are going to tell them 27
      2.   Stick to the plan 27
      3.   Work the audience 28
      4.   Body Language and Mannerisms 30
      5.   Questions 30
      6.   End on a high 32
   CHAPTER 4 – ACHIEVING COMPETENCE 33
      1.   Getting objective feedback and presentation skills assessment ... 33
      2.   Analysing your assessment to identify development needs 37
      3.   Create a development plan 41
      4.   Success Factors for Implementing your Plan 44
   CHAPTER 5 – MAKING A CASE 47
      1.   Creating your case 47
      2.   Create the presentation 50
      3.   Lobby the decision makers 54
      4.   Delivering your case 54
      5.   Dealing with objections 54
      6.   Case Presentation Assessment 55
   CHAPTER 6 - BARRIERS TO EFFECTIVE PRESENTATIONS 57
   CHAPTER 7 - FURTHER READING 60

Synopsis

Being able to present yourself and your ideas to others is the key to the door of success. No one gets anywhere in life on their own, we all need the help of others. Some of us are lucky enough to be 'born' into environments designed to help us 'get on' in life. Others have natural influencing skills which make them 'stand out' but for most of us we only stand out, because we stand up. We have to work on 'selling' ourselves in the market place. This means being able to;

- ✓ present ourselves as a person with something to offer
- ✓ communicate about ourselves
- ✓ make a compelling case for what we want

This book is one in a series which focus on helping you the reader to optimise your interpersonal communication skills. It uses the Action Learning philosophy to enable you to develop your presentation skills. It starts with an explanation of how World Class presenters prepare and deliver their presentations. This is followed by an opportunity for you to assess your current level of presentation skills and create a Personal Development Plan setting out the actions necessary for you to become a competent presenter. Presentations are an integral part of every ambitious person's communication tool kit. Being able to present competently is an essential skill for everyone who has the ambition to be a leader.

Other books in the series are:

- ✓ Communication Skills – Tool Kit
- ✓ Managing Difficult Relationships
- ✓ Interviewing Skills
- ✓ Negotiating Win/Win Solutions
- ✓ Developing Others
- ✓ Managers as leaders

Acknowledgements

I would like to acknowledge the great debt of gratitude I owe to Professor Reginald (Reg) Revans, the founder of the Action Learning movement. We met in 1974 when he was planning his first Action Learning programme in GEC. At the time of our first meeting I had recently transferred from line management into a management development role. I was very aware that mature managers did not respond well to 'teaching' and was searching for ways of creating learning opportunities. Over lunch Reg shared his ideas with me and I was sold; thirty-five years later I am still a convinced action learner. He introduced me to Alan Lawlor who pioneered Own Job Action Learning in the West Midlands and the three of us created Action Learning Associates (ALA) Intentional in 1980 to promote the application of Action Learning. My relationship with Reg continued until his death in 2003.

I would also like to acknowledge my good friends Malcolm Farnsworth, John Cooper and Richard de Laat.

Malcolm, who as Principal of the Marconi Staff Development Centre in Chelmsford, gave me the chance of a new career in management development which I have pursued for a very stimulating thirty-five years.

John, who I worked with at The Dunchurch College of Management, is a natural 'action learner' as anyone who has used or experienced the marvellous business simulations he created will testify and generous to a fault with everything he did. For me John is one of the unsung heroes of Action Learning and deserves to be recognised as such.

Richard for his encouragement and editing of this book; without Richard's guiding hand it would probably never have seen the light of day'

Finally I would also like to acknowledge the many hundreds of participants and clients from around the globe who I have learned with and from over the years. It has been a great privilege to know you, thank you all.

George P Boulden - May 2016

Presenting Professionally- Introduction

We are all used to communicating, talking with other people. We do it all the time, it's natural, we don't even think about it. Making a presentation however is different because we are no longer a 'member of the pack' we are its leader. This change in status creates two problems:

1. It's stressful being up front. Virtually every one has been or will be, called on at one time or another to make a presentation. Whether this is a formal occasion, updating management on the progress of project X, or informal, making a speech at a friend's wedding; for most of us our maiden speech is a stressful experience. Why? It's simply because we are standing out from the crowd. During our early years we are taught to 'follow' now we are being asked to 'lead'. It's an entirely different situation; we are on our feet on our own in front of an audience who expect???

2. What to say and how to say it. Unlike a conversation, which is interactive, when making a presentation we are alone. In a conversation, we can learn the needs of others through discussion and respond appropriately, in a speech there is no opportunity to do this; we have to find out in advance what our audience will expect from us and plan to meet these expectations if we are to be successful.

So it's a problem and we need to solve it. We learned ride a bike, tie our shoe laces, persuade others to give us things we want et al, we can also learn to do this. There are three components in the learning equation; the 'process' the steps that we must follow to be successful, the 'skills' we need to develop to and the 'behaviours' we must unlock to empower ourselves to make a professional presentation.

This book looks at Presentation as a four step process;

1. Plan
2. Rehearse
3. Deliver
4. Achieving Competence

In step one you will learn how to create a winning presentation. In step two you will learn how to prepare yourself to deliver it and the practical things that you need to do on the day to ensure your success. In step three you will learn the secrets of audience control. In step four you will use your real time experience to identify the areas you may need to improve and receive guidance on how to do this in practice. Learning is an iterative process; we do something, we reflect on what we have done to identify areas for improvement. We use this information to modify our approach to the task and try again and again until we become competent. By following the learning process set out in this book you can become a Professional Presenter.

Note. There are two main types of presentation;

- ✓ those concerned with giving information and
- ✓ case presentations

The main difference between the two is that with 'information' presentations we are seeking to inform the audience with a 'case' presentation we are seeking to persuade the audience to do something. Whilst the process and skills required are the same in both types of presentations the structure of the material is different. If you are creating a presentation to give information you will use the approach described in chapter 1 for a case presentation you will use the methodology set out in Chapter 5.

So let's get started.

Chapter 1 - Plan

Your task is to make a 'successful' presentation. Successful means you satisfying the needs of your audience and feeling good about your performance. Yes it is a performance, welcome to the stage. In this chapter we will show you how to create the story, write the script and prepare your 'props'.

1. Decide your purpose

Why are you making this presentation? What do you wish to achieve? It takes time and effort to prepare a presentation properly so it's important on the one hand to get value from your investment and on the other to provide a meaningful experience for your audience. To do this we need to answer the following questions:

What, specifically, is the purpose or core idea of the presentation?

For example, to persuade the CEO to approve $50,000 of additional funding for project X (See chapter on Case presentations for more information) , to inform customers about the new upgrade to product Y, to get some feedback on your idea fir changes in the way we pay our sales people… etc. Write down in no more than one sentence the reason for the presentation and the outcomes you expect.

What message exactly should the audience have received when the presentation is finished?

For example; we need two more staff, we should buy three of product X…

How, precisely, will I know if I have achieved my objective?

For example; I have a signed order for five units of X, the audience will be fully engaged in the closing discussion...

2. Identify your audience

Once we are clear about *what* we want to say, the next step in developing a winning presentation is to define the needs of the audience. They are your 'customers' in this context and you are there to satisfy their needs. To be an effective communicator it's necessary to make your message appealing and interesting to them. Typically, audience needs fall into a four categories:

- ✓ Those who come to hear what you have to say – they are interested in content
- ✓ Those who are curious about you as a person – they would like to get to know you
- ✓ Those who have to be there – they need to be encourage to become engaged
- ✓ Those who can influence the outcome – they need to be persuaded

Therefore, for the presentation to be effective it is vitally important to take into account the needs of these different groups in the 'content and style' of your presentation. To do this we need to answer a number of questions:

Who will (or who should) be in the audience?

For example will it be internal or external people? Will they have different interests? For example will there be both technical and financial people there? What is their level of understanding of the topic? These things are important to know because they determine the 'level' of your presentation. For example it would not be appropriate to use a lot of technical content in a presentation to a largely non-technical audience but to satisfy the 'technocrats' you could provide a 'handout' for them to take away.

How large will the audience be?

This is important because it will determine things like room layout, potential for audience participation, the need for technology like microphones and visuals etc.

3. Define the context

Defining the context is concerned with identifying;

- ✓ how long the presentation will be
- ✓ when it will take place and
- ✓ where it will take place

This information can be gathered by asking the following questions:

How much time is available for the presentation?

Thirty minutes is about the longest that most people can maintain maximum concentration. If your speech is scheduled to last longer than this some form of activity must be built into the presentation to prevent the audience 'switching off.' These activities can take many forms:

- ✓ Coffee/tea & rest breaks
- ✓ Question and answer sessions
- ✓ Demonstrations
- ✓ Forming the audience into small discussion or 'buzz' groups

What time of day will the presentation take place?

In the morning audiences are at their most attentive and can assimilate quite large amounts of data; always assuming that they haven't been entertained on too lavish a scale the night before!

After lunch their attention tends to wander; the larger and more liquid the lunch the greater this effect. This implies that:-

- ✓ The amount of 'hard' material should be limited in these sessions.
- ✓ A greater emphasis should be placed on 'entertainment' than in the morning.
- ✓ Involving the audience in some sort of activity, for example working on a sample problem or case study is a good way to maintain interest.

In the evening, after a long day's work, the audience is normally tired. This means that the same rules as for the afternoon apply, only more so. A limited amount of difficult material, a high entertainment factor, and if possible some activity like discussion groups or hands on experience of using equipment etc. should be included in the session.

4. Write your Script

All 'theatre' is scripted and it is from the script that actors learn their lines; the more studious the learning, the better the performance. Presentations are just another form of theatre in which you are the actor. Now the purpose of the presentation is clear the audience and timing defined, the next stage is to decide what you are going to say. Start by;

Gather information about the topic of the presentation.

Start by listing the key points you would like to make. Don't be concerned at this stage with the sequence of ideas, or even if they seem to be 'silly', or, 'impractical'. This exercise is designed to use the power of the unconscious mind so we must allow ourselves to be open and creative and note down all the ideas that come to us. In some cases, it may be helpful to hold a group brain storming session to illicit additional facts, ideas, and possible approaches. For more information about brainstorming see Thinking Creatively

(DK Essential Manager Series) by George P Boulden at this Amazon link.

Over the next few days carry out any additional reading, fact finding, data collection that the initial 'rough' notes suggest might be necessary. Review the notes and sort out the ideas;

- ✓ identify main headings
- ✓ discard irrelevant material
- ✓ allocate the remaining points to one of the main headings

Review the headings and sub headings and decide which are:

'Must know' - Vital points necessary to achieve the aim of the presentation
'Should know' - Desirable for the audience to know these, but not essential
'Could know' - Relatively unimportant, but often interesting and entertaining
Write what you are going to say

Note. This is time consuming and hard work. However it is essential to achieve a professional performance on the day.

The structure is simple and the same for all presentations;

Dynamic start, interesting middle and summarise at the end'

'Tell them what you are going to tell them, tell them, tell them what you told them'

Start with the introduction:-

- ✓ Who are you
- ✓ Why are you making the presentation
- ✓ What will you speak about – key points
- ✓ How long will it last and when they will get coffee
- ✓ How will you handle questions

- ✓ Ask the audience if they have any questions at this stage

Write the body of the presentation using your key points as 'anchors'. Gather any missing information and organise in a logical sequence.

Try to use metaphors, analogies and 'sensory' based language to reinforce your points. Sensory based language is important because it personalises what you are talking about. For example 'we have done well, but I **feel** we can do better and would like to … I was very **sad** to hear that Jane will be leaving us at the end of the month to … ' I would like to say how **grateful** I am to Bill for the … If you are presenting the monthly report you might start with something like 'The good news is that whilst we are not 'exactly drowning in orders, things are better'…and if there has been a problem with the format of the figures you might say something like 'I know you don't like the new format the finance people are using, 'someone said it was like reading the FT before breakfast'! So I have tried to produce a simpler version…'

Consider the end; what message(s) do you want to leave the audience with and how best to stress these.

- ✓ Summarise what you have said highlighting the key points
- ✓ Tell them what you would like them to think or feel now. I hope you have:
    - ➢ enjoyed my presentation
    - ➢ found it useful
    - ➢ enough information to enable you …
- ✓ Thank them for coming
- ✓ Ask if they have any questions
- ✓ Close

Do nothing for a couple of days.

This allows the subconscious mind to work on the problem and develop ideas.

Review and edit what you have written

You should now have a written text with an introduction, a list of key points, the content of what you want to say about each one and the 'close the message you want to leave them with.

5. Create Visuals

Research indicates that around 80% of the information we take in comes through our eyes, so visual aids are an important part of your presentation because they:

- ✓ Enable the audience can both see and hear the message
- ✓ Make a presentation more dynamic; the screen provides an alternative point of focus which allows the presenter to switch the attention of the audience from themselves the screen and back again.

As a general rule for information based presentations it is best to make one slide for each of your key points with sub text for the things you are going to speak about. For a travelogue one would use pictures of the places we would like to speak about and so on. These visuals provide prompts when you are on your feet and if you have learnt your text you will be able to speak directly to the audience without the use of notes.

The following is an example of the slides we use in our Presentation Skills Workshops.

Slide #	Slide Image	Slide sub text
Slide 1	 **EFFECTIVE PRESENTATIONS** • ESTABLISH THE CONTEXT • PLAN THE CONTENT • CONTROL THE ENVIRONMENT • PRESENT THE TALK	

Slide 2	
	ESTABLISH THE CONTEXT
	• CLARIFY OBJECTIVES
	  What do I want?
	• DEFINE THE AUDIENCE
	  Who are they?
	  What do they want from me?
	• SPECIFY THE SETTING
	  Where will the talk take place?
	  When will it happen?
	  How long do I have?	

Slide 3	 **PLAN THE CONTENT** • GET THE FACTS • ORGANISE THE FACTS • PLAN VISUAL AIDS • WRITE OUT THE TALK – metaphors & analogies • LEARN & REHEARSE • 'KEY POINT' NOTES	

Chapter 1 - Plan　　　　　　　　　　　　　　　　Presenting Professionally

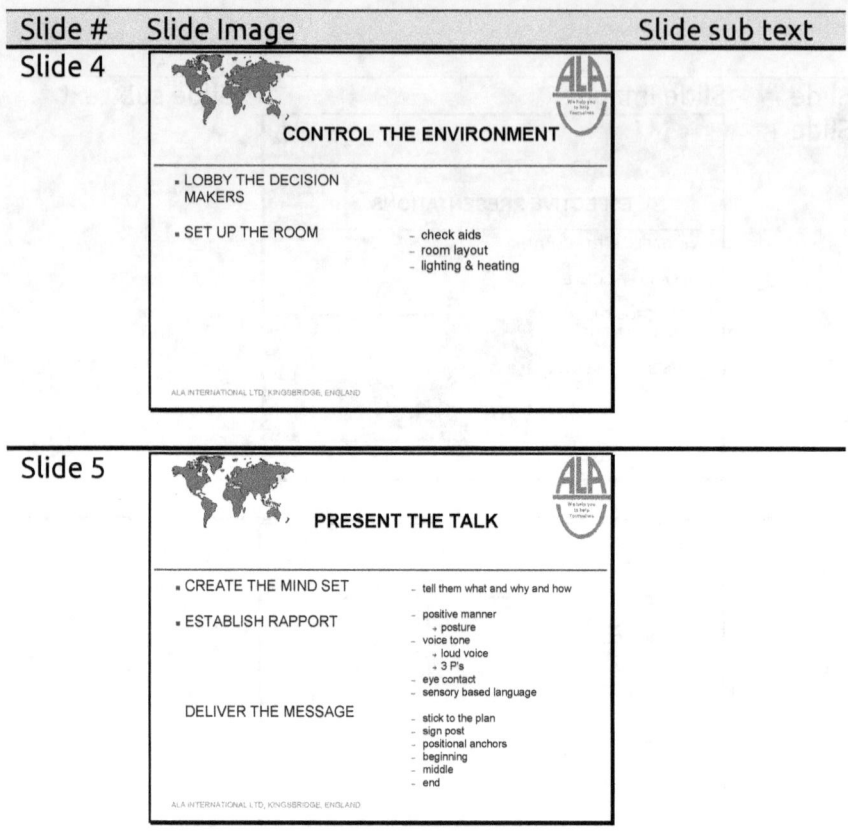

Note. The main stay of most business presentations is the laptop, the video projector and of course the screen. It's always worth checking at an early stage that the equipment you require will be on hand for the presentation.

Chapter 2 - Rehearse

Now you are the actor and like the actor, you have the script and the props, all you have to do now is learn your lines.

There are four steps in this stage;

1. Learn your lines
2. Learn to manage the fear
3. Practice, practice, practice
4. Create your environment

1. *Learn your lines*

We need to learn our material like an actor because knowing the material means;

- ✓ We can 'speak from the heart'. The written word is not the spoken word; the written word comes from the head, the spoken word comes from the heart.
- ✓ It's all about emotions; you must believe what you are saying; if you don't believe it, I won't believe it either.
- ✓ We can 'work the audience' we feel how the audience is responding to our message and can amend the message in the light of the feedback.

So how do we learn? It differs, different people learn in different ways. I have student who can read an A4 page once and talk about it. I personally need to read the script a number of times over a few days and then practice using the Key Points as an 'aide memoire'. How you learn is not important. The goal is to be 'script free' on the day, able to present from the heart.

2. Create the conditions

Learning to deliver your speech means developing you're communicating skills. Speaking formally to a group is not the same as chatting with friends. We are alone, exposed on the platform and for most of us this is a daunting experience and so it should be. We are responsible for ensuring that the people who have come to listen to us have a worthwhile experience and we achieve this by delivering a professional presentation. This means creating the conditions where you feel you are speaking to friends and they feel valued and informed. We achieve this by;

- ✓ Developing rapport; establish your right to be there
- ✓ Providing useful information in an interesting way
- ✓ Working with the audience; being responsive to their needs

3. Rapport

Rapport is the portal through which we must pass to open the door for effective two way communication. It is the 'essential' first step to a relationship with another person where both are able to speak openly even about things on which they may not agree because there is 'trust' in the relationship; both expect an outcome that will be mutually beneficial. Being able to create rapport is the key to success in both individual and group communication. The performance review meeting will go well if we both feel that the discussion is 'honest' and for the benefit of both parties. The audience at the monthly review meeting will be receptive if they feel that what is agreed will benefit them. Rapport building is also an essential part of successful mass-media communication. The first few pages of the book determine whether we feel it's worth reading; the first few minutes of the film, concert or show are crucial to our involvement and enjoyment of the performance. Without rapport there is no relationship.

Rapport

Rapport is a natural process for both humans and animals, it is nonverbal and ritualistic. Two dogs meeting for the first time on their afternoon walk begin the process of relationship building by looking at each other. As they get closer one will normally sit down whilst the other will approach. As they get closer together the approaching dog will normally start to sniff the sitting dog. If all goes well the sitting dog will stand and circle the other dog, if this is OK they accept each other. They may then just walk on or decide to play a bit.

People are the same, when we meet someone for the first time we evaluate them, initially, as with the dogs, to see if they pose any threat to us. If they do we take whatever defensive action seems possible / appropriate. If they look interesting we start by saying 'Hello'. Our initial judgement about others, as with the example of the dogs, is non-verbal. We gather our 'first impressions' through our eyes, ears and senses and use this information to condition our response; positive if we like what we see and negative if we don't. Assuming we like what we see we then move actively into the process of developing rapport. We do this by matching our body language with that of the other party using tone of voice, eye movements, facial expressions, posture and body movement, breathing etc. This matching or mirroring is in its natural state sub-conscious but is clear to anyone observing the behaviour of others. Once we have 'rapport' we have open channels for two way communication. Since we all are naturally capable of building rapport, we have a powerful skill that we can use consciously to start or improve our communication

Overcoming our barriers

If rapport is natural and all of us have the ability to develop it, what's the problem? For some people there is no problem because they believe that everyone they meet has some value; successful sales people are a good example of this. However most of us only develop rapport with people who we value; usually people who are like us. With others we communicate but without rapport there is always a barrier. To become a successful communicator we must break through these self-imposed barriers. Effective presenters achieve this by starting the dialogue with areas of common interest;

- ✓ If you know some the people you can acknowledge them in your introduction and where appropriate introduce a little humour, 'It's nice to see Bill here again, hope you don't fall asleep this time!
- ✓ A few words about something relevant to all, like the weather, the journey, the coffee, lunch etc.
- ✓ If the session starts with coffee the presenter has a chance to meet at least some of the people and can use these contacts in their opening remarks.
- ✓ Asking if anyone has any questions they would like to ask before the presentation starts.

The aim is to establish some relationship between you and the audience something that will make them feel good about you and you feel good about them.

Maintaining rapport

Once rapport is created we must work to maintain it. We do this by watching for non-verbal signals for lack of interest. Things like people looking at their watches, reading notes, moving in their seats not blinking etc. If you spot any signs of lack of interest, you need to do something different. The easiest way to re-focus the audience is either to change tack or ask a question. If you are going through a budget for example and you see that people are losing interest the simplest approach is to say something like. "Look, this is very detailed and it's in the notes, why don't we just skip to the end and look at the conclusions? And do that.

Keeping them awake can be difficult. No matter how interesting your presentation is as a piece of work delivered in a monotone from the script it will soon put even the most tolerant audiences to sleep. We have three main tools we can use to 'spice up' our performance.

- ✓ Voice
- ✓ Questions
- ✓ Body language

Voice – When we are listening to someone our minds are tracking the sounds and as soon as the mind believes it is tuned into the rhythm it starts to go to sleep. So to keep the mind awake we need to continually change the three P's Pitch, Pace and Pause. By changing the Pitch of our voice, speaking more loudly or more quietly stimulates the mind. Changing the Pace at which we speak means the mind must process more or less data and Pausing means it loses the signal, so it searches for it and we stay awake.

Questions also stimulate the audience because they may be required to answer them. This is where rhetorical questions come in very handy. For example asking, 'How many of you know the profit potential of our new product'? This will certainly wake them up and you can avoid any embarrassment by answering the question yourself; 'Of course you all do, otherwise you wouldn't be here'!

Body language - You are alive, so you should be moving, walking about the stage, not hiding behind the lectern. Point at your visuals when you are talking about them, point to yourself when speaking about how you feel, embrace your audience when you speaking about their feelings... but don't overdo it. Walking randomly about the stage can be distracting to the audience and is to be practiced with care. People are also distracted by constant random hand and arm movements; restrict them to those necessary to re-inforce your key points. You are presenting with your body; be yourself. Remembers this is 'show business' if you enjoy the experience your audience will enjoy it too.

Eye contact – Making eye contact with the audience is crucial to your success as an entertainer. People look at our faces when we speak and they assess the truth of what we say by the openness of our face. If you ask someone a question and they look away when they answer we 'know' that the answer will not be the truth. The expression on your face must reflect what you are saying, sometimes smiling, sometimes, serious, sometimes sad. Making eye contact with small audiences is easy, you can see everyone. With large audiences this is not possible so look for people who 'stand out' and focus on them as if you are talking to groups in the audience with a leader. Make sure that you look 'around' the audience, front, back, left, and right so that everyone feels that at some stage you are looking them.

Humour can be very helpful in maintaining rapport but it can also backfire. I my experience jokes are out but amusing anecdotes relevant to the material and the occasional 'off the cuff' comment work well.

4. *Learn to manage the fear*

We are all motivated by our needs and controlled by our values. Individual needs determine what we seek and seek to avoid, cultural values determine what we see as acceptable and unacceptable behaviour. These things are 'programed' into us in childhoods using the simple process of reward and punishment. When we do 'good' things we are 'encouraged' and feel 'good' about ourselves and others. When we do things that are unacceptable to those around us, we are 'discouraged' and are unhappy. This process is ongoing throughout childhood and over time we learn to associate feelings of comfort, security, happiness with 'good' behaviour and feelings of discomfort, insecurity, unhappiness leading to stress with discouraged behaviours. In most societies children are taught to fit in and belong, not to lead, leading is for others! So whilst sitting in the audience is fine, making the presentation is not because it requires us to lead. This is a suppressed behaviour so we feel stressed. This stress is natural as was said earlier because we are being pushed out of our comfort zone. To manage this stress we have to 'empower' ourselves to lead; we achieve this by;

- Getting permission to change the programme from people who we see as competent presenters
- Repetition – unwanted behaviours are suppressed by repetition; I see this with my grandchildren but never realised I was doing it with mine! To undo the process we empower the desired behaviours by repeated reward.

Change is always risky; we are going into the unknown so we try to limit the risk by talking with people who have done what we want to do successfully. This is a natural process that we all use when we want to do something that we have been 'programmed' not to do. It's simple and it works, we take someone else's success and use it to give ourselves 'permission' to succeed. See out book Change; become a Winner for more detail.

5. Practice, Practice, Practice

Familiarity with the message can be gained by repeatedly reading the presentation out loud. The use of visuals should also be practised during these 'dry runs'. In addition it is possible to check facial expressions, voice tone and body language by either (i) tape recording or videoing the rehearsals or (ii) practising in front of a mirror. For very important presentations colleagues should attend the practice sessions to give (constructive) feedback on performance. Practising your presentation ensures that the:

- Timing of the presentation is right.
- Impact is correct, and the main points are properly emphasised.
- Visuals work smoothly and are appropriate.

➢ Use of notes is kept to a minimum during the actual presentation.

Condense the presentation to key points and write them on one side of blank postcards.
Each card should be numbered and the writing should be large enough from one or two paces away. Don't forget to number your prompt cards, just in case you drop them on the day!

This move away from the full script is necessary to avoid the temptation to actually read from it during the 'live' presentation. If this happens the delivery invariably sounds stilted and pedantic. Delivering the message from memory and using key points for guidance ensures that the presentation is lively and spontaneous. With well-chosen visuals to act as prompts, even the 'key point cards' may be dispensed with allowing for a "seamless" performance. Note. If a report on what you say is to be distributed after or even before the presentation the written speech can be edited and then used for this purpose.

As a last' safety' check – review the script and ensure that it supports the core ideas you want to communicate and meet the needs of the audience.

6. Appearance

So far we have focused on content and presentation however there is a third factor which is key to our success on the day; this is our appearance. The way you as the presenter dress, your general grooming, hair style etc., are all part of the message that will be read by the audience. A suit and tie means 'formal' but take your jacket off and roll up your sleeves it means 'let's get down to business'. Open neck shirt and jeans means 'informal' relax and enjoy. The aim of the professional presenter is to get their message across which means choosing the style of dress which is appropriate to the occasion. Inappropriate dress causes 'noise' which interferes with the building of rapport and the transmitting of that message. To 'fit in' you match expectations, to challenge you mismatch'.

7. Create your environment

This is your show; you are not only the author and the leading actor you are also the choreographer responsible or both the on and off stage environment. This involves finding out about and organising the venue well before the presentation. The following points are important:

Before the Presentation

- ✓ Obtain a map showing the venue and work out how to get there.
- ✓ Establish that the room is large enough for our purposes.
- ✓ Ask the venue to arrange the layout that is required. (e.g. 'U' shape classroom style etc.)
- ✓ Make sure in advance that any equipment you require and any other special needs like extension leads extra power points if you plan to demonstrate equipment… is available.
- ✓ Check whether there is the audio equipment that you need to support your presentation.
- ✓ Check the lighting and familiarise yourself with the controls.
- ✓ Agree your coffee breaks etc.

On the Day

- ✓ Arrive early and ensure that the earlier requests have been complied with.
- ✓ Check <u>all</u> equipment and visual aids. Ensure everything works, all aids are clearly visible, and that you are familiar with the operation of the equipment.
- ✓ Ensure that lighting is adequate and that you have control over it - this is particularly important when using certain visual aids (e.g. 35mm projectors.)
- ✓ Ensure that you have control over the heating in the room - if it is either too hot or too cold people will find it difficult to listen to the presenter.
- ✓ Check the acoustics of the room; make sure you can be heard clearly. (Allow for the fact that a room full of people can absorb a lot of sound energy.)
- ✓ Find out where the toilets are and the evacuation procedure JIC.

Meet and greet the audience as they enter the room, if coffee is laid on mix and chat with them. This has two main benefits:

1. It establishes rapport between you and the audience by breaking down any barriers through making personal contact.
2. It establishes the venue as your territory and increases your authority over the proceedings.

Move positively to the speaking area; pause; look around at the audience; weigh them up; smile; look enthusiastic, take a breath and, begin to speak.

Chapter 3 - Deliver

Finally, we are on stage and the focus of everyone's attention. Our first task is to achieve a state of rapport with the audience. This is **essential;** not only does it create the conditions for open communication but it is the conduit through which you as the speaker 'tap into' the energy of your audience. Everyone with experience of presenting will tell you that 'rapport' is the key to success. Once you have the audience 'with you' you are invincible. You feel their energy surging through you, willing you to give the performance of a lifetime; without their energy you are drained before you have even begun.

1. **Start by telling them what you are going to tell them**

    - Hi! My name is… I am…
    - My purpose today is… to tell you about some exciting research we are doing into…
    - I will begin by giving you some background… then…
    - My presentation will last about 20 minutes and there will be time for questions afterwards…
    - Are there any questions before I begin? And no, I can't do much about the coffee!

2. **Stick to the plan**

During the preparation phase you have developed a logical structure aimed at helping the audience understand and (hopefully) accept our core message(s). It is important therefore to deliver the presentation in line with this carefully prepared plan, this means:

- Starting with a firm and confident greeting followed by an outline of the topics to be covered.

- ✓ Moving through each topic in a logical manner and in the sequence outlined in the introduction.
- ✓ Ending with a concise summary of the ground that has been covered and leaving the audience in no doubt about what they are expected to do next.

3. Work the audience

Make eye contact

Command attention by making eye contact with the audience; maintain this eye contact to obtain feedback on their response to what you are saying. Only by looking at the audience is it possible to determine whether they are bored or interested, asleep or awake, as you communicate with them.

Use voice control

One of the things that most irritates an audience and helps to lose their attention and sympathy, is when they cannot hear the presentation. The speaker <u>MUST</u> speak so that everyone present can hear what is being said. If this requires the use of a microphone you must ensure that you are fully conversant with its use and the limitations they can impose. Volume in presentations comes from using the diaphragm adequately <u>not</u> from straining the throat; if a presenter must address large audiences on a frequent basis it may be appropriate to receive some voice training or buy one of the many books available on this subject.

As was said earlier a flat delivery in a monotone will have the effect of destroying rapport. Using your voice to create variety in speech patterns is necessary to overcome this potential danger and the key factors are;-

Pause

A short silence before a key word and at the end of sections in the speech adds drama and emphasis to what is being said. Pausing is particularly powerful at the beginning of the presentation, before we start to speak and at the end, before we begin the conclusion.

Pace

If the pace is too slow the audience get bored; too fast and they cannot understand what is being said. For the purpose of presentation changes of pace are necessary to hold interest. However, the fastest speech in presentation will be slower than that used in normal conversation. Beginners especially need to be aware that what initially feels a slow pace when giving a presentation is quite fast when one is listening to it.

Pitch

The up and down modulations of the voice are key in producing the variety in sound that keeps an audience interested in the message. A flat delivery makes it difficult for people to listen; though of course wildly fluctuating tones also have the same effect.

Emphasise

By putting extra effort into key words the presenter helps the audience by highlighting the most important parts of his/her sentence and again provides a variety of sound to help keep the listener 'tuned in.'

Enthuse

Enthusiasm is infectious. If the presenter appears interested in and enthusiastic about their subject these positive feelings will spread to the audience. Thus a positive approach should be adopted from the start of the presentation. We should march boldly to the speaking position; pause; look around weighing up the audience for a few moments; smile at them; take a deep breath and start to speak clearly and positively. Paradoxically even if the presenter is 'acting' this positive calm role and in fact feels nervous and uncertain, the act of taking up the role does actually cause these feelings to lessen and then disappear.

4. Body Language and Mannerisms

Movement, gesticulations, posture and mannerisms can positively aid understanding, be neutral, or distract from the message. Jingling change in pockets; excessive scratching of noses; saying, 'now' or 'um err' at the end of every sentence; leaning on desks or podiums; wildly gesticulating arm movements etc. are generally inappropriate. Other actions which do not distract the audience are permissible. Some presenters like to stand behind a podium or table when making a presentation. It makes them feel more comfortable and allows them to control their body movement more easily. Holding the podium can stop excessive arm movements and it provides something to do with the hands. Such devices however create a barrier (physical and psychological) between the presenter and the audience and thus hindering the establishment of rapport between the two parties - unless the presenter is very nervous they should be avoided.

5. Questions

Questions from the floor help build rapport between the speaker and the audience. They allow for points of interest to be clarified and discussed and for the audience to participate in the meeting. If the presentation is over 15 minutes long some sort of activity, like question and answer sessions, are advisable to hold the audiences interest. If our presentation is of interest to the audience they will want and expect to ask questions. To deny them the opportunity will create frustration and barriers between us and the group. Often, however, although people in an audience want to ask questions they are inhibited from doing so. It is one thing to be part of an audience, quite another to have the spotlight of attention turned on you and risk the embarrassment of being seen as asking a foolish question. It is the case though, that the more questions are asked the easier it becomes for individuals to contribute. It follows that if the presenter wants questions he needs to plan for them. Three main methods are available:-

- ✓ Have a plant ' in the audience with a prepared question.
- ✓ If there is a chairperson prime them to ask a question.
- ✓ Ask yourself a rhetorical question. e.g. "Actually one thing I do get asked quite a lot is ….." and then answer it.

When someone asks you a question respond by repeating it. This gives you time to think about your answer and ensures that the whole group has heard it.

When answering a question you as the presenter should:

- ✓ Address your remarks to the audience as a whole not just to the individual who asked it.
- ✓ Remain standing this gives a greater physical presence over the audience, who are sitting thus enhances the presenter's authority.

If you don't know the answer to a question you can;

- ✓ Throw it open to the audience and ask for their views.
- ✓ Ask the questioner to explain what he/she means in more detail in the hope that they will answer it themselves.

However

As the presenter must never pretend to know the answer; if you don't know the answer simply say so and promise to find out the information and get back to the questioner as soon as possible.

Members of the audience don't always ask questions in order to get more information, sometimes they ask questions to attack the presenter's credibility or to prove to the group how clever 'they' are. Techniques for dealing with hostile questions include:

- ✓ **Never argue.** The presenter should simply note the difference of opinion and offer to discuss the matter with the questioner fully after the presentation has finished.
- ✓ **Ask a question.** Answer a question with a question, draw out the other person and regain the initiative.
- ✓ **Broaden the discussion**. Ask the rest of the audience for their views; don't get trapped in a one to one debate.
- ✓ **Stay assertive.** The presenter should not become either aggressive or passive but remain in control by using the three step 'assertiveness' technique – I understand that you ... However, I feel that ... and therefore I suggest ... The voice tone should be firm and even, the body posture should be upright and relaxed, and the point in question calmly stated without anger or apology. For more information on assertiveness and other behavioural tools see our book 'Communicating for Success'

6. End on a high

Now it's time to tell them what you told them. The start of any presentation is important because it sets the tone for what is to come. The end is crucial because it's what they will remember.

- ✓ Summarise what you have said highlighting the key points
- ✓ Tell them what you would like them to think or feel now. I hope you have:
- ✓ enjoyed my presentation
- ✓ found it useful
- ✓ enough information to enable you ...
- ✓ Ask if they have any questions
- ✓ Thank them for coming
- ✓ Close

Chapter 4 – Achieving Competence

Everything we do in life is a learning opportunity but this only becomes a reality if we are prepared to use it. The child learns that the stove is hot not by touching the stove but through the pain that comes for the burn afterwards. To learn we must not only do, we must, also be prepared to objectively reflect on the experience and willing to commit to doing what is necessary to improve.

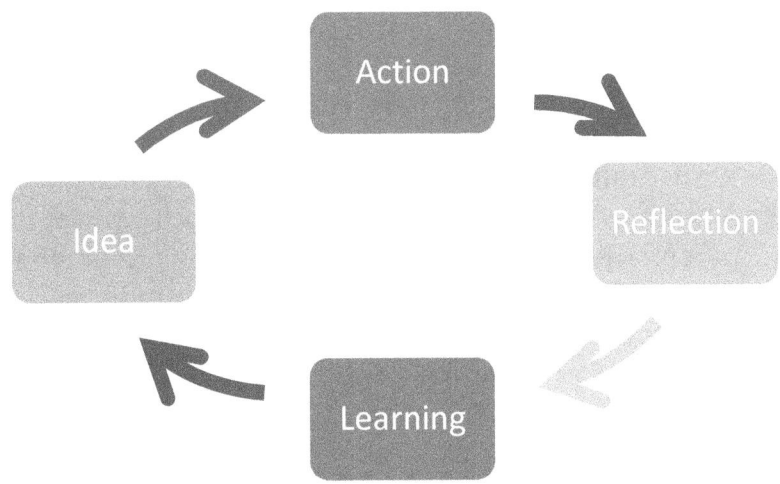

1. **Getting objective feedback and presentation skills assessment**

After each presentation make an honest assessment of what went well and what areas require improvement. There are two ways of getting objective feedback:

Ask the audience what they thought about the presentation. This can be done by;

- ✓ Circulating 'happy' sheets at the end of the presentation
- ✓ Running a question and answer session
- ✓ Informal 'chats' with members of the audience and colleagues
- ✓ Discrete 'eavesdropping' during coffee breaks.

The sorts of questions to consider are:

- ✓ Were some sections too long and others too brief?
- ✓ Was the technical element too highbrow or too simplistic?
- ✓ Did the audience follow the arguments?
- ✓ What points had the most/least impact?

Self-assessment - To do this objectively we need;

1. A self-assessment 'model' based on the process and skills demonstrated, in this case, by 'professional presenters'. We use this information to create
2. A process for self and peer assessment which involves the potential learner in delivering, in this case, a presentation. This 'real time' activity is then assessed to identify any areas for improvement.
3. Where such needs exist a development programme is created to enable the presenter to achieve their desired outcomes.

All human activity can be looked at in terms of the process and skills demonstrated by people who are competent in that activity. This information can be used to help others who are currently less able to improve. For presentations the process and skills needed to be successful are defined by the expectations of the audience. What they see, hear, think and feel about the presentation determines their assessment of you as the presenter. Our research shows that the way audiences assess presentations falls into the following broad categories:

1. Objectives – If the audience doesn't know the reason for the presentation it will not understand its content.
2. Structure – Beginning, middle and end; we understand information when it is presented in a logical way
3. Content – Audiences expect to listen to something that has some value for them. Why waste time listening to someone who does not have anything interesting to say?
4. Impact – If it makes no impact on the audience they will not listen
5. Delivery – Audiences need to feel involved; that the message is for them
6. Visuals – The audience expects them to be clear and complement what is being said
7. Control – Audiences expect the speaker to be able to control the audience. Answer genuine questions yes but not to be side tracked or bullied by strong members of the audience
8. Assessment – What was in it for me? Audience always assesses a presentation that is why they are there; we need this assessment for self-improvement.

We have used these categories to create a method for objectively assessing presentations and presenters.

Presentation Skills – Assessment

Categories	Points for assessment	Comment	Score
OBJECTIVES	Was the purpose of the talk clear? Did it meet the audience expectations?		
STRUCTURE	Did the talk have a logical flow? Was the 'correct' amount of time given to each topic? Did it have an opening, middle, and end?		
CONTENT	Was the information meaningful & valuable? Were metaphors and analogies used? Was there a good 'mix' of sensory-based language?		
IMPACT	Did you feel involved from the start? Did the speaker develop a rapport with the audience? Were the audience interested in what the speaker had to say?		
DELIVERY	Did the speaker use his/her voice well? (e.g. pause, pace, pitch) Did the speaker's physical movements add to the presentation? Did the speaker keep to the plan? Did the speaker use his/her notes well?		
VISUAL AIDS	Were they relevant? Easy to follow? Too many or too few?		
CONTROL	Was the audience properly controlled? Were questions handled well?		
ASSESSMENT	Did the speaker achieve his/her objective? What impression are you now left with of his/her message? Are you clear what happens next?		

Score:- Good – GD, Satisfactory - SAT, Needs Improvement - NI

Now it's your chance to assess yourself and create a benchmark. Please consider the last presentation you made and write comments against each question in the comment box. When you have responded to all of the question in a box, review your comments and see whether you are Good, Satisfactory or Need improvement and enter your score accordingly. If possible ask two or three people who have heard you speak to also complete and assessment form.

2. *Analysing your assessment to identify development needs*

Having completed your assessment, the next step is to analyse it, what do the results mean and what can we do about them? To help you with this task we have three simple case studies based on some of the more common needs we have identified when training presenters. Please read the following cases before you start your own assessment.

Case 1.

Categories	Points for assessment	Comment	Score
OBJECTIVES	Was the purpose of the talk clear? Did it meet the audience expectations?	Yes No	NI
STRUCTURE	Did the talk have a logical flow? Was the 'correct' amount of time given to each topic? Did it have an opening, middle, and end?	No No – too general – more facts No end – just stopped	NI
CONTENT	Was the information meaningful & valuable? Were metaphors and analogies used? Was there a good 'mix' of sensory based language?	Not very Poor Poor	NI
IMPACT	Did the speaker develop a rapport with the audience? Were the audience interested in what the speaker had to say?	To some degree – good personality Yes but could have been more so	SAT
DELIVERY	Did the speaker use his/her voice well? (e.g. pause, pace, pitch) Did the speaker's physical movements add to the presentation? Did the speaker keep to the plan? Did the speaker use his/her notes well?	Yes Good – Open and confident What plan? What notes?	SAT
VISUAL AIDS	Were they relevant? Easy to follow? Too many or too few?	No Yes but not relevant	NI
CONTROL	Was the audience properly controlled? Were questions handled well?	Good rapport yes	SAT
ASSESSMENT	Did the speaker achieve his/her objective? What impression are you now left with of his/her message? Are you clear what happens next?	What objectives? Don't know what the message was No	NI

Score:- Good – GD, Satisfactory - SAT, Needs Improvement - NI

These scores indicate that whilst this presenter developed good rapport with the audience their planning of the presentation was poor and needs improvement. We would recommend that the individual use the Presentation Skills Development Plan to prepare for their next presentation.

Case 2.

Categories	Points for assessment	Comment	Score
OBJECTIVES	Was the purpose of the talk clear? Did it meet the audience expectations?	Yes Only partially Content OK	SAT
STRUCTURE	Did the talk have a logical flow? Was the 'correct' amount of time given to each topic? Did it have an opening, middle, and end?	Yes Yes Yes, but lacked impact	SAT
CONTENT	Was the information meaningful & valuable? Were metaphors and analogies used? Was there a good 'mix' of sensory based language?	Yes, but lacked dynamism No – very 'dry' No	NI
IMPACT	Did the speaker develop a rapport with the audience? Were the audience interested in what the speaker had to say?	No – had little contact Would have been if it were presented better	NI
DELIVERY	Did the speaker use his/her voice well? (e.g. pause, pace, pitch) Did the speaker's physical movements add to the presentation? Did the speaker keep to the plan? Did the speaker use his/her notes well?	No – quietly spoken, monotone Very little movement Yes NO – he hid behind them	NI
VISUAL AIDS	Were they relevant? Easy to follow? Too many or too few?	Yes Yes About right	SAT
CONTROL	Was the audience properly controlled? Were questions handled well?	No – not involved None asked	NI
ASSESSMENT	Did the speaker achieve his/her objective? What impression are you now left with of his/her message? Are you clear what happens next?	NO Boring No	NI

Score:- Good – GD, Satisfactory – SAT, Needs Improvement – NI

This individual had a well-planned presentation but was unable to deliver it with impact. This is a typical case of 'speech fright'. This person needs more exposure to making presentations supported by lots of rehearsals beforehand to give them confidence. The experience will be much more beneficial if they can find themselves a coach, someone experienced in making presentations who will help them with their rehearsals and support them on the day.

Case 3.

Categories	Points for assessment	Comment	Score
OBJECTIVES	Was the purpose of the talk clear? Did it meet the audience expectations?	Yes Only partially	SAT
STRUCTURE	Did the talk have a logical flow? Was the 'correct' amount of time given to each topic? Did it have an opening, middle, and end?	Yes – as far as it went No Opening and middle OK but no end	NI
CONTENT	Was the information meaningful & valuable? Were metaphors and analogies used? Was there a good 'mix' of sensory based language?	Yes Yes Yes	SAT
IMPACT	Did the speaker develop a rapport with the audience? Were the audience interested in what the speaker had to say?	Yes Yes	SAT
DELIVERY	Did the speaker use his/her voice well? (e.g. pause, pace, pitch) Did the speaker's physical movements add to the presentation? Did the speaker keep to the plan? Did the speaker use his/her notes well?	Yes No No No – what notes!	NI
VISUAL AIDS	Were they relevant? Easy to follow? Too many or too few?	Not very Yes Too many	NI
CONTROL	Was the audience properly controlled? Were questions handled well?	No speaker too responsive No – verbose replies	NI
ASSESSMENT	Did the speaker achieve his/her objective? What impression are you now left with of his/her message? Are you clear what happens next?	No – didn't finish Confused Needs to be done again	NI

Score:- Good – GD, Satisfactory - SAT, Needs Improvement - NI

Good delivery spoilt by lack of discipline. The presenter lacked time planning, had a tendency to ramble and was verbose in answering questions. The comments indicate that this person needs to review the way they plan their presentations using the Presentation Skills Development Plan and rehearse beforehand to ensure they can deliver the message within the allotted time. The visuals need to be re-thought.

Now it's your turn to create a benchmark. Please complete the following table:-

Strengths – the things I am good at	Weakness – things I need to improve

3. Create a development plan

Having decided what you want to work on the next step is to create a plan. The plan allows you to visualise what you need to do to achieve your desired improvements and provides a useful vehicle for both control and sharing. Your plan needs to set out what you will do, by when and how you will assess your achievement. The following example is from case 1

Case 1

PERSONAL DEVELOPMENT PLAN

Name ...Tom Brown.................... Start Date ....2nd June....... End Date....End July.............

Title of Project: - Becoming as Professional Presenter
Purpose: What do you want to achieve through the action? To develop my self-confidence when giving presentations. I would like to achieve a 'good' rating for delivery from the majority of the audience
Current Situation: Where are you now? I plan my presentation well but am unable to deliver with impact. I am so stressed by the situation that when I stand up I have forgotten what I'm about to say. I need to develop my self-confidence through practice. I need someone to help me. Presentation is an essential part of my job; I am determined to be good at it.
Actions: What actions do you plan to undertake? By when? (Be specific about dates) Ask Richard for help, agree first rehearsal for next week and organise video – Today. Use results of first rehearsal to agree detailed development plan – 14th June Work on development plan with more rehearsals. Live presentation, ask audience for feedback – 26th June Review results with Richard and decide on next steps – end July Note. Our experience shows that for most people a concentrated period of supported practice like the one outlined here will be sufficient to give the learner the self-confidence they need.
Resources: What resources do you have to help you achieve your outcome? How can you make best use of them? My regular monthly presentation. Richard. My video which I can use to record my practice session for analysis. The benchmarking form from this manual
Outcome: What are you aiming to achieve? How do you want things to be different? I will be a competent presenter; seen buy colleagues one who presents useful information in a logical and interesting way.
Results: How have things turned out? What have you learnt from the experience of working on the project?

Now it's your turn. Complete the following Personal Action Plan for yourself.

PERSONAL DEVELOPMENT PLAN

Name.......................... Start Date.................... End Date............................

Title of Project:
Purpose: What do you want to achieve through the action?
Current Situation: Where are you now?
Actions: What actions do you plan to undertake? By when? (Please be specific about dates)
Resources: What resources do you have to help you achieve your outcome? How can you make best use of them?
Outcome: What are you aiming to achieve? How do you want things to be different? What specifically will you see and hear when you have finished that you don't see and hear yet?
Results: How have things turned out? What have you learnt from the experience of working on the project?

Tips when creating your Plan
1. Start by listing the activities. The things you will do to achieve your development goals.
2. Identify key events. For this plan the most logical key events will be your actual presentations.
3. Create realistic time scales
4. Review to ensure it is do-able - Be realistic. Don't set your goals too high or they become de-motivating, too low or they have no value.
5. Don't try to do too much - Go for little and often. Remember the old saying 'How do you eat and Elephant? One bite at a time!
6. Use objective measures – things that can be objectively assessed. Things like, time, quantity, dates, results etc.
7. Create milestones, key events which you can use to track your progress.
8. Share it with someone. Sharing a plan makes it more powerful. You are more likely to see it through if you have someone who is going to ask you how it's going!
9. Use your plan to monitor your achievements.
10. Don't be afraid to update it if things change. It's a live document and should reflect where you are and where you are going.

4. Success Factors for Implementing your Plan

There are a number of factors which influence the success or failure of a Personal Development Plan:-

The main requirement is discipline; being committed to doing the work. Personal Development plans are like diets, easy things to draw up but very difficult to stick to. This is basically because what we are now reflects our values, things we seek and the things we seek to avoid. I weight 100 kilos because I like good food, enjoy a social drink and would rather watch TV or read a book in the evenings that go to the gym. If I really wanted to be 75 kilos I would have to change my life style, deny myself those things I like and start doing things that I don't like.

One of the most powerful motivators for people is fear of looking a fool, which incidentally is why so many people don't like making presentations! And, whilst this is of itself a negative emotion it can be and is used positively to help people who want to change. It is the core driver for self-help groups like Weight Watchers, Alcoholics Anonymous, Stop Smoking and thousands more. Such groups have good results because the majority of members don't want to let each other down. You can also use this emotion to help you win through. If you can find else who wants to develop their presentation skills and agree to work together coaching and supporting each other. This is very effective because neither party wants to appear foolish in the eyes of the other. The next best thing is to find a coach. Someone you respect who has some experience of presenting and ask them to help you by giving feedback and support. This is also effective because you are no longer alone.

Don't be too rigid about the plan

Be prepared to make changes as you go along. The main thing is to stay focused on your desired outcome. You want to be a competent presenter do what's necessary to make this happen.

Continuous Improvement

My father used to say 'Every day in every way, I get better and better and better'. This not literally true of course, what he really meant was that every day provides the opportunity to get better. So what will you do to get better? Maybe the following questions will help you to decide!

1. What is the one thing that if you did it or stopped doing it would have the beneficial impact on your personal or business life?
2. Looking at the relationships you have with others what is the one thing that if you did it or stopped doing it would have the beneficial impact on their lives?
3. What would you like to do with the rest of your life? What do you need to do now to begin the journey?
4. If you were working a three day week what would you do with the other two days? What's stopping you?
5. Who is in the 'driving seat' of your life? Are you content with the direction of travel?

Things only get better if we make them better

Chapter 5 – Making a Case

The goal of a case presentation is to persuade some third party to 'do' something. We do this all the time 'informally'. The basic process is simple; it's all about 'trading'. We offer the person who has something we want, something we have in exchange for them giving us what we want. The child who would like to watch television before going to bed may offer to go to bed immediately the programme ends. The teenager who wants to go 'clubbing' promises to be home by midnight. The inventor seeing investment offers the potential investor the opportunity to become rich. Clearly in the first two examples this is an informal process, no facts or figures are necessary but the 'inventor' needs to make a 'business case'. In this chapter we explain how to create a compelling business case using the 4P's methodology.

1. **Creating your case**

Define your objective

As with 'information' presentations the first step is to define your objective(s). For example it might be that you are seeking to:

- ✓ Get funding for your invention
- ✓ Convince your boss that you should work from home three days a week
- ✓ Be promoted
- ✓ Persuade your partner that it would be good to buy a new car
- ✓ Convince your parents that they should fund a gap year for you to go to Asia
- ✓ …

The important thing at this stage is to be clear what outcome you are seeking from your presentation. This could be funding, an agreement on action(s), the acceptance of an idea et al…

Identify your audience

Start by finding out who will be there and their role. Normally, in case presentations, the audience will be made up of the curious, decisions influencers and decision makers (buyers); the latter are the most important.

Who are the Decision makers & Decision Influencers?

Decision makers can say yes or no to our proposal. They have the power to make things happen directly so, if possible, case presentations should be made to the decision makers. If there is just one decision maker you will want to pitch the 'sell' to them. If however there are more than one possible buyer you may well want to select the most likely buyer as you target, without losing sight of the needs of other potential buyers.

Decision influencers can 'assist' the sale if they like what you are offering but they cannot authorise it. If they approve it they must refer to someone else for a decision. This referral could involve anything from putting a case on your behalf to the decision maker to arranging access for you to approach him or her directly. Making a 'pitch' to an influencer is always a weak option because one has little control over how they will represent our arguments to the decision maker. Clearly, there is no point in making a case presentation to someone who is not a decision maker or influencer.

What do decision makers want from a proposal?

Whilst the goal of the case from the seller's perspective maybe the same, all cases are different because the 'buyer' is different; thus what 'ticks the boxes' for one is not the same for another. Decision makers tend to feel compelled to act when they perceive that the offer is a 'solution to a problem they are trying to solve' or when offered significant opportunities; something what will enhance their status in some way.

To build a compelling case, therefore, we need to:

- ✓ Be able to frame our reasons for wanting action to be taken in terms of solving a known problem or grasping an opportunity
- ✓ Understand why the decision maker finds themselves in the current situation
- ✓ Determine if the decision maker believes that the current situation does need to be addressed. If he / she does not, then the presentation needs open with a focus on persuading them that there is a problem that needs to be tackled before offering solutions.

Quantify the problem or opportunity

Having identified a problem or opportunity the next step is to carry out some form of measurement to determine how 'big' a problem or opportunity it is. Quantifying the problem in this way makes it much easier to gain acceptance that action needs to be taken to address it. This almost always means measuring the *financial implications* of the problem.

For example, a manager of a parcel delivery service might accept that not giving van drivers cell phones creates communication problems. If however, it could be shown through the analysis of journey logs, that the cost of not having the technology to quickly re-route vans costs X thousand pounds a year, he / she will be more inclined to act.

Clarify the underlying needs

In order for a solution to be accepted it must address three areas of need:

1. the needs of the business
2. the personal needs of the decision maker
3. the needs of the presenter

These needs often, but by no means always, overlap. If we want to win our case, we must develop a proposal that aims to satisfy all three. There is no point in suggesting an approach that will be of great value to the business if it threatens the personal needs of the decision maker. This may not be 'right' but it is a fact of life and winning cases always take this 'political' dimension into account.

Develop a solution

It is now possible to develop a solution. This involves:

- ✓ Listing at least three possible options. Note. Doing nothing is always an option to consider. In most cases it can be used to demonstrate that it is not an option as doing nothing will only make matters worse thus legitimising the case for the other options!

- ✓ Identifying the pros and cons of each option relative to the three sets of need and their cost implications.

- ✓ Picking one solution –Now it's time to identify your 'best fit' option. This will already be obvious from your comparison of the business and the decision maker(s) needs with the benefits of the three options. All you need now against the be obvious from

2. *Create the presentation*

Now we know what we would like and we know who we are pitching to. To be successful the content must reflect the needs of the decision maker(s). So we need to find out what factors will influence your potential customer's decision to 'buy'; what will they look for in your presentation. If you are selling an idea, some buyers will look at the creativity of your proposal, others will look at the quality of your research, others will want to find out how committed you are to your proposal...

If you are working with others this should be done as a team by 'brainstorming', desk research, assembling ideas etc.

Using the 4P's format

Having done the ground work the next step is to put the information together using what is called the **4p's format.** This starts with an introduction which outlines the ground to be covered and goes on to cover the key topics in the following sequence:

Introduction

Position

An overview of the background to the current situation: how we got to where we are today.

Problem

A discussion of why where we are today is a problem. Be sure to highlight any quantifiable data that has been gathered and in particular to ensure that the financial costs of the problem are clearly identified.

Possibilities

Outline the possible courses of action. List the benefits and downsides associated with each of the possible choices.

Proposal

Put forward your preferred option. Highlight the benefits to the business and to the decision maker; be sure to include a financial cost/ revenue argument. Acknowledge the more obvious objections and give the counter arguments. Be honest about any drawbacks to the proposal and spell out how 'downside' can be managed. The audience will simply not believe us if we try to maintain that our case is perfect. By bringing any weaknesses of the proposal out into the open we meet the expectation that there is a 'catch' somewhere and this will greatly enhance our credibility with the group.

Now take your data and put it into the 4p's see example below:

Case Study

Background
Company XYZ manufactures sports equipment it has been in business for many years and has enjoyed a reasonable level of success. It was recently taken over by an investment Company who feel that there is an opportunity to expand the business. They have appointed a new CEO who is targeted with achieving 20% growth over the next five years. He has identified a sales opportunity and has recruited five additional sales people to exploit this and the orders are flowing in. This has created a bottleneck in the Order Entry Section which is unable to process all of the increasing flow of orders even with maximum overtime. The manager feels that the only option is to hire more staff and has booked a slot on the next regular management meeting to make her case.

Introduction
Good morning! As you all know I'm Jill and I run the Order Entry Section. I have a problem which affects all of us and I would like to share it with. I have a proposed solution and hope that you will see this as a practical response to a critical situation and approve it...

Position
I am in charge of entering sales orders onto the computer system and have found that we have a growing backlog of orders. My people are desperately overworked, putting in lots of overtime, we just can't cope and it's getting worse.

Problem
The problem is that the business has grown. We have five new sales people and are now trying to bill half a millions pounds worth of orders with the same number people I had before and we are falling behind at the rate of £25K a week.

Possibilities
To improve things we could re-write the software to make data entry easier but IT advise me will take at least 18 months.

We could ask the sales people to do some of the order entry work but they have always refused point blank to help out in the past and there is the issue of the impact of this on their bonuses and the loss of sales time. We can hire another data processing person.

Proposal
I see hiring an extra person as the only realistic solution. Without this additional head the department as a whole will miss the sales figures for the year by £250K. Another operator will solve this problem. It will cost £30,000 all up which will more than be offset by the additional £250K orders books and a saving of £1,000 a month for overtime. I have spoken with HR and we believe we can have someone in by the end of the month. Here's the authorisation form and I'd appreciate it if you could sign it off by the end of today, thank you."

Without the extra staff the department, and by implication the CEO, will not meet its business goals by a quantifiable amount. Only the CEO can have an impact on the situation by authorising more manpower - the problem has been transferred to him. The CEO may or may not care that the Order Entry section is over stretched but will certainly care that the lack of capacity is endangering his ability to achieve his business targets especially having recently recruited five additional sales people to ensure that these targets are met!

3. Lobby the decision makers

The chances of success when giving a case presentation are greatly enhanced by holding informal meetings and discussions with key personnel *before* the presentation takes place. This type of activity helps people to understand the issues involved in the case and 'softens up' the decision makers before a formal presentation takes place. Lobbying in this way prepares the ground for the case presentation by:-

- ✓ gaining additional data about underlying needs
- ✓ ensuring a common understanding of the issues (if not agreement on them) is developed
- ✓ allowing objections to be identified early, and thereby giving time for strong counter arguments to be prepared
- ✓ reducing the possibility that an idea will be rejected simply because its 'new'

4. Delivering your case

Case presentations are delivered in the same way as standard presentations but the following factors need to be given special consideration.

5. Dealing with objections

In a case presentation it is helpful to get all questions/queries/objections out on the table before you begin to answer them. This makes it is possible to adopt a strategic approach to the queries raised rather than deal with the points on an ad hoc basis. This is done by responding to the first question asked at the end of the presentation by saying something like:

"Do you have any other queries about my proposal?"

It is useful to write the questions on a flip chart if you have one in not on paper. Once you have all the questions look for clusters; for example there maybe a number of questions about costs. If you have the answers, answer, if not say so and offer to find out. Work through the questions and seek agreement that you have either answered the questions or will find out. If there are issues that need to be resolved schedule another meeting.

Diplomatic language

In making case presentations and answering questions it is important to establish a calm, logical tone to the proceedings as well as, on a personal level, using large helpings of tact.
For example:-

If you say to your boss that a current practice is "wasteful and stupid" but he has been presiding over it for five years you may well irritate rather than persuade. Better then to emphasise the positive aspects of potential "efficiency improvement" than the current negatives of waste and neglect.

Other 'irritators' include the uses of such phrases as; "I think that's very fair" - Therefore if you disagree you are by implication unfair; "This is a very reasonable proposal" - anyone who disagrees is therefore unreasonable; "I would have thought that was made clear in the presentation" – are you stupid! Etc. Irritators by definition annoy people and people who are annoyed stop listening, if people don't listen they can't be persuaded and the case presentation will fail.

Always remember, this is a 'sale'; what you say is important but so is how you say it and how you look!

6. *Case Presentation Assessment*

Presenting a case is also a learning opportunity. However, whilst the methodology used is the same as that set out in the previous Chapter the planning process is different so we recommend that you use the Case Presentation Skills – Self Assessment form below to assess your learning needs.

CASE PRESENTATION SKILLS
ASSESSMENT CHECK LIST

		GOOD	OK	NEEDS IMPROVEMENT
OBJECTIVES	Was the purpose of the case clear?			
STRUCTURE	Did the case have a logical flow? Was the 'correct' amount of time given to each point? Did it have an opening, middle, and end?			
CONTENT	Was the information meaningful & valuable? Were metaphors and analogies used? Was the case clearly made?			
IMPACT	Did the speaker develop a rapport with the audience? Were the audience persuaded to approve the desired action(s)?			
DELIVERY	Did the speaker use his/her voice well? (e.g. pause, pace, pitch) Did the speaker's physical movements add to the presentation? Use of notes?			
VISUAL AIDS	Were they relevant? Easy to follow? Too many or too few?			
CONTROL	Was the audience properly controlled? Were questions handled well? Did the speaker use the assertiveness technique?			
ASSESSMENT	Did the speaker achieve his/her objective? What impression are you now left with of his/her message? Are you clear what happens next?			

Chapter 6 - Barriers to Effective Presentations

There are a number of generic problems, which reduce the impact of a presentation and sometimes lead to complete disaster. These are;

1. Objectives. Mutual needs not clearly understood; what do they want to hear and what can I deliver it? Without a clear understanding of the needs of the audience and the presenter's knowledge, skills and motivation to satisfy these there is little chance of a successful outcome for either party.

2. Poor planning. Not taking the time to prepare is an insult to your audience to go into a presentation not properly prepared and they will not forgive you for it. The aim of the presentation is to deliver a specific piece of information; upcoming changes in the Health and Safety legislation for example, to a group of people, the management team, in a short time, 20 minutes. To do this effectively one needs planning and rehearsal

3. Inability to develop rapport. Two-way communication only takes place after one has developed rapport with the audience. Communication is not simply a matter of speaking; it requires the receiver to hear and understand the message for it to be two-way. The presenter must 'make the audience want to listen to what they have to say if he/she wants them to understand the message. When you are on the stage the audience is the most important thing in your universe, you must make them believe in your sincerity if not the rightness of your ideas.

4. Poor use of time. Time is an inelastic resource. From the moment you stand up, until you sit down again, every second counts. Say what you have to say and shut up. Brevity is good. If you can take less time than you are allocated do so, let them break early for lunch and you are a star.

5. Lack of clarity, It's not only important to speak clearly, it's important to think clearly. The ideas you are communicating must 'hang together' in a logical way otherwise your audience will not understand them.

6. Poor opening or close. These are the two most important parts of your presentation. The audience will have decided within the first minute if you are worth listening to, so make the first 60 seconds count. The thing they take away with them will be the summary of what you said. Make sure it's the message you want them to take away.

7. Poor visuals. Poor visuals are worse than no visuals because they distract. Visuals are useful because the add variety to a presentation but they must be relevant and professional.

8. Being over confident and not valuing the audience. Believing that as you're the 'expert' in your subject and they will listen to you. No they don't and if you antagonise them they will not value what you say.

9. Being unable to look at the audience. In many societies children are taught that it is rude to 'stare' at others. Which is true, however when you make a presentation people expect you to look at them, if you avoid eye contact they tend to assume that you are not telling the truth. So it's necessary to look at your audience to demonstrate your sincerity. It's also necessary so that you can see how they feel. Research indicates that people who are actively

listening to someone blink every five to seven seconds; if they stop blinking they are going to sleep!

10. Fear. I leave this to last because it is the most difficult of the barriers to overcome and the most common. Virtually everyone who is asked to make a presentation at least in the early stages of their career feels stress. This is natural because we are being asked to step outside the comfort and anonymity of the group and become the focus of attention. This is risky for us, if things don't go well we will lose status in the eyes of our colleagues or friends. So we have to make sure things don't go wrong by planning and rehearsing. With practice we become proficient. We get used to presenting and some of us even come to enjoy it. We learn to manage our fear so that in time it becomes only the stress of anticipation, or as they say in the theatre, 'first night nerves'. For more information about Speech Fright see at this link: '10 Causes of Speech Anxiety that Create Fear of Public Speaking' by Gary Genard.

Chapter 7 - Further Reading

If you have found this book useful you might also find some of the following books interesting;

1. For an insight into human behaviour I recommend Dr. Thomas A. Harris is the author of *I'm OK – You're OK*, the 1969 bestseller based upon the ideas of Transactional Analysis by <u>Dr Eric Berne</u>. ISBN 0-06-072427. If you find this interesting you may also like to read 'The Games People Play, by Dr Eric Berne ISBN 0-345-41003-3

2. In the same genre but more focused on 'rapport' skills is NPL, How to Build a Successful Life by Richard Brandler, Alessio Roberti & Owen Fitzpatrick, published by Harper Collins, ISBN 978-0-00-749741-6

3. For a deeper understanding of values, I suggest 'What Matters Most' by Hyrum W Smith, published by Franklin Covey Co. ISBN 0-684-87256-0

4. For an entertaining insight into the real world of influencing I recommend the book 'When I Stop Talking You'll Know I'm Dead by Jerry Weintraub, Rich Cohen and George Clooney, Published by Hachette Books ISBN 978-0-446-54815-1

Books George has written on Action Learning and related topics

The following books are published by ALA International. They are available on our web site www.ala-international.com and from **Google Books** and **Amazon** in Epub, PDF and paperback formats.

Books about Action learning

Applications of Action Learning – describes the philosophy of action learning and its applications. ISBN 978-0-9560822-4-4

Own Job Action Learning – describes how Action learning can be used in individual development programmes. ISBN 978-0-9560822-0-6

In-Plant Action Learning – explains how the philosophy of Action learning can be used to deliver organisational change. ISBN 978-0-9560822-3-7

In-Plant Action Learning Teams, Participants Guide – This Guide is designed to help In-Plant teams to self-manage and facilitate their own learning; available from ALA International.

Facilitated Learning – describes how the process of facilitation is used to develop participants in Action Learning sets. ISBN 978-0 - 9560822-9-9

Books about Personal Development

Managers as Leaders - This book show how management and leadership combine to ensure the effective delivery of the task. ISBN 978-0-9560822-2-0

Managing Difficult Relationships – examines the reasons for difficult relationships and provides a 'framework' for negotiating win / win solutions. ISBN 978-0-9560822-5-1

Change; Become a Winner - I believe that life is not a rehearsal, it's a journey and you can change it. If you would like to do something different with your life this book is for you. ISBN 13 978-1503185401, ISBN 10:1503185400

Books about Productivity

Values & Style; the Key to Productivity – The common denominator in performance improvement in organizations, is managing style. The things that stop people doing the best job they can stem from 'them and us' attitudes. These are based on cultural values and determine the way human beings perceive their roles and relationships within hierarchies. This book explores the nature of values and style and how they impact the operating effectiveness of organizations and societies.

Re-Engineering the Workplace – This book describes the Japanese approach to productivity with practical examples on how it can be applied in practice.

Useful web sites for Action Learning

Action Learning is a worldwide network. The following are some useful contacts in the Action Learning world please go to this link: "The 7 Best Resources for People who are Trying to Learn How to Unlock Hidden Potential with Action Learning" by George P. Boulden.

Please use this link to find our books on Amazon.

I will be very grateful if you will take a few minutes to write a review on this book while you are here. Thank you.

George Boulden

www.ingramcontent.com/pod-product-compliance
Lightning Source LLC
Chambersburg PA
CBHW070333190526
45169CB00005B/1872